Inspirational WINDS

Inspirational WINDS

Words That Blow The Mind and Calm The Soul

DIRDURA WYNN

XULON PRESS

Xulon Press
2301 Lucien Way #415
Maitland, FL 32751
407.339.4217
www.xulonpress.com

© 2023 by Dirdura Wynn

All rights reserved solely by the author. The author guarantees all contents are original and do not infringe upon the legal rights of any other person or work. No part of this book may be reproduced in any form without the permission of the author.

Due to the changing nature of the Internet, if there are any web addresses, links, or URLs included in this manuscript, these may have been altered and may no longer be accessible. The views and opinions shared in this book belong solely to the author and do not necessarily reflect those of the publisher. The publisher therefore disclaims responsibility for the views or opinions expressed within the work.

Paperback ISBN-13: 978-1-66285-897-0
Ebook ISBN-13: 978-1-66285-898-7

THIS BOOK IS DEDICATED TO

My mother Barbara Rembert- passed 11-2017
Lebarrion Rembert- my brother
Lequita Ceaser -my only remaining sister
Vanessa Rembert- sister -passed in 2012
Clarence Rembert Jr.–brother -passed in 2022
Felicia Rembert-sister passed in 2007
Quinones Rembert – my brother
Dwayne Rembert- my brother

Introduction:

The words in "Inspirational Winds" were conceived in the mind of the author and put on paper, the contents have delighted many for over 20 years. If you have encountered snuggles, and fears, you will enjoy reading Inspirational Winds. The message of guidance and encouragement are for children as well as adults. The words are intentional, the feelings that they provoke are real. It is also filled with a variety of artwork. Take a walk through the art gallery, beautifully done by Sabrena Wynn and Sheila Wynn. The author hopes that you dive in and enjoy the read. Inspirational Winds, let it blow your mind and encourage your heart.

Table of Contents

Words of Inspiration for the Very Young and Young at Heart - Black girl - An Intro to me xiii

Section I xv
The race of life 1
The seed 2
Compare 3
Balance 4
Divine portrait 5
Wise woman 6
The blessed one 7
Peace 8
Stop the violence 9
The cycle 11
Oh, what a friend 12
A healthy fear 13
Family Day 14
Teachable 15
Faith 16
Parting the mind 17
Simplicity 18
Spiritual, not physical 19
God's natural flow 20
Have a heart 21

Section II - Personal Words of Gratitude from the Heart .. 23
To Lizzie M. Wynn 24
Mother 25
To my mother and friend 26

Coming together 27
Daddy 28
Cherish the love 29
Precious moments 30
The taste of home 31
Wonders of life 32
No matter what.. 33
Dearest mother.. 34
Twins 35
We are one (You are flesh of my flesh and bone of my bone).......... 36
A Father's Day wish for my brother 37
Raging storm 38
Cry if you must... 39
Teens In the 90's 40
Drop a tear/and rise with praise 41

Section III - It's all about love **43**
Riley my love 44
Frank 45
My love 46
When I say "I love you"... 47
Great father and husband.. 48
Being married is an oxymoron..................................... 49
A thought on Mother's Day.. 51
Trusting in the Lord.. 52
My prayer 53
Let them wonder 54

Section lV - From My Children **55**
David -The great calm 56
From the pen of Sheila - Fluttering thoughts...................... 57
Rachel- Love grows like a garden 58
Nicole–Dearest mom - 10 things I want you to know you do 59
Sabrena- A word of appreciation 60
Chelsea–You bring passion 61

Section V **63**
Footprints of Jesus 64

Introduction:

The wind's doors 65
The clouds do cry 66
Sprinkles of salt 67
The flat land speaks 68

Inspirational winds to the very young and young at heart.

BLACK GIRL
(A POEM, AN INTRODUCTION TO ME)

Not from royalty, no silver spoon at my birth- bumpy, roads hard and good times met me. Some of my loved ones have said goodbye to life. But here I am, still here, pushed to the side, not chosen in a crowd. No matter how I screamed, pick me!–out loud.
No one cares about that snub nose, short hair black girl-
Hum, my mom was black and my dad too-
As a part of my mom and dad, my sisters and brothers, are a beautiful bouquet of shades of black, brown and light cream. So, I stem from a family, like that. Not a bronze chic or tented by the sun- Just a black girl created by God and born from my mom and dad. Not from Mexico, or Germany, though my name might be-listen, if you uproot a Sycamore tree from its home and plant it in East Africa, would it still be a Sycamore Tree? Just saying, my name is Dirdura, pronounced Dil-tura, that's me, not Diddo, or Deidara. But I'm not angry, this is true; I celebrate me, and you celebrate you. It is The Lord that have quietly worked with me. My Lord and master have taken a frail twig and have given me a song. The songs that I sing have traveled through time. Traveled through scary close my eyes and pray times and times that I prayed that I wouldn't lose my mind. Songs of good times, yes, I am blessed that you are around. Songs of placing my loved ones into the cold hard ground. Song of spring days when bouquets bloom spraying their aroma and iridescent in an open field or a drab room. Yes, I sing these songs at the hue of light from the morning sun, at noon, dusk and my songs greet

the harvest and new moon at night. I thank him, The Mighty LORD for sculpting my mind and guiding my tongue and I will work for him, until he says my work is all done. Yes, this is me, this black girl is rooted and grounded in The Lord and for every will be.

Section 1

THE RACE OF LIFE

Life is a race.
Listen to your parents and take heed
to their pace.
Why?
Because if you run too fast
your race won't last, and you will end
up in a four-cornered case.
Beware of people that say, "do as I say
and not as I do,"
remember, they are to be an
example to you.
But don't fret or fear cause
The Lord is always near.
So, cleave to God's hand and move forward
because the race is on.
But this race is not to the swift of feet,
but to those that honor the Lord,
and are spiritually strong. Find yourself where God's people are- two is
better than one.
Whether the race is near or far, no
matter where you are
his path is straight and true, his word
will also guide you.

The Seed

God is the seed of life and the maker of it.
The greater becomes the lesser and the lesser becomes the greater, who can tell?
When we are not, someone is.
For a man to live, he must be planted into the womb,
unless he spills and dies.
But the spilling of flower seeds brings
forth an abundance of flowers.
God is the creator of us all.
And he trust man, to carry out his divine plan.
Bless his holy name.

Compare

A strong Christian is likened to a tree planted deep into the earth. Our trunks wear and our branches do brake but our roots travel deep into the earth. Though the storms of life rages and winds of time beat against our foundation.

When evil chop, and with words cut us down, we hide in him that is where we can be found. Not a physical place but working in his vineyard sometimes without a sound. Quiet as an Oak tree, brave and strong; knowing the Lord is near, we are never alone. His mighty Spirit shelters us from quiet rage and fierce storms.

Balance

Too many leaves on the ground look tacky, but just a few remind us of God's beautiful season. Too many birds chirping disturbs the ears, But harmonious melodies from a few songbirds calm the soul. The reddest Carnal awakens the eyes, but the song of the Three-Wattled Bellbirds can pierce the ears. Too many raindrops overtake a house, but spring showers bring forth fragrant rosebuds, and waters the seeds that sprout life.

We must enjoy the showers and take cover when the tide rises. Who can prevent it or say to the sky, don't overtake us?

Too many sun rays will inflame the ground, houses mount as rubble and the hills of flames send animals out to save their life, even the rarest creature will come out of hiding. But just a kiss from the sun rays feeds the foliage that covers the ground. God has tampered all of nature together to be pleasing to Him, and respected and cared for by man. What an amazing God and an awesome plan. A delicate balance, in the hollow of his hand.

Divine Portrait

There is no form that can hold him.
His character can't be contained.
To the lowly, He is their mighty tower.
By his countenance, He gives strength and worth. To the troubled in spirit, He is that calm and welcoming river, saying drink and live.
To the remorseful man, He is a forever calling voice and stretched out hands, saying "Come, come, and be made whole again."
To the lost, He is the path to follow and guiding light.
To the sick, He is that great physician, He offers the cure and hope for life.
But not so to the hearts that are dark and whose faces are many. To their lowly, they will be crushed and blown from their space with a wave of His hand. To their troubles rivers will rise higher than they can bear. To their blind, they will stumble, and a cliff will be set in the way. In their despair, desolation will follow–
But nonetheless, He is GOD, and there is none like Him, above- on or beneath earth. When we repented turn and obey Him,
He will comfort us and be our God and we will be His people.

WISE WOMAN

A wise woman honor and fears the Lord.
She has peace for garments and
prosperity wrapped about her waist.
The garment of godliness, and
love for the family that the Lord has
given to her.
Her garments are peace, in adversity,
love, and understanding in uneasy times.
And calm admid pain.

The Blessed One

Through you, God has allowed life to flow.
You are the carrier of the seed that is planted by man.
Through your nurturing, and guidance, babies grow.
You are the link that we need to carry babies as a seed.
You are a woman.
You are the blessed one.

PEACE

May the peace of God cover your mind with comfort, like the soft light of the harvest moon, keep the darkness at bay.
Look to The Lord, that provides all your needs.
And even if you must cry,
It's okay when saying goodbye.
But let peace overcome your fears and know in your memories
your loved one is always near.

Stop The Violence

Stop the violence, I tell you.
Stop the violence, or it will stop you.
Can't you see your parents' faces
as they run to the streets?
Contoured lines upon their face.
They are afraid of what they will
meet, what they will meet when
they run to the street.
Afraid of seeing their daughter
or son face down in the street, so off the run.
You see, they heard a loud sound that rang the night, and the scream of neighbors, which gave them an awful fright. They ran to your bedroom and called but you are not there, then another sound filled the air. The pounding of their hearts and the rattling of their bones as they rushed out to the street —so sad and feeling all alone.
Tears streamed from bloodshot, tired eyes and down their worried faces.
Can't you see them? Can't you see as they wonder, "Oh, my Lord,
what shall I do?" "What shall I do to relieve this grief?"
My child is now deceased."
Dead for the price of maybe a few words.
Or maybe a wink of an eye or a slight tilt of the head.
But what if they had won, another family to grief would have to succumb, to days of sleepless nights; and wanting to even the score. I must even the score, this is what violence demand because my child breathe their last breath, not to breathe any more. Think, think and think some more, If we all put our

weapons down and follow the God's plan, this would save our young and old ladies and our young and old men.
So, stop the violence-
The blessing is for you and me; because, from the hurt of violence we will be free.
Trying to make things right by doing wrong puts violence on a throne.
So, let's plant seeds of forgiving and healing and allow God's word back in our homes, and take violence off the throne.

THE CYCLE

Mama had a baby before she was wed,
later dad did it,
he and mama wed.
Well, dad was not a man that stayed home,
he left mom and me all alone.
But when he was there, he and mom would fight,
sometimes from morning till night.
I would stop my ears and run to my bed
and spread the blanket from my feet to my head.
I would say from time to time, my dad's life would not be mine.
As the years passed, I moved out on my own, for lack of better words, I began to sing the same song.
My lady had a baby, she later became my wife.
As the cycle goes, we fought sometimes from morning till night.
I lifted my hands and screamed to the sky.
Who will stop this cycle? I would cry.
Who will prevent our children from going down the same path?
Yes, their future I dread, so I sat with my wife.
We sat and prayed to the Lord, for instructions on what to do.
The answer is simple and knowing this is true, your children will engage in what they see you do. I said in my mind "Hmm, that's true." I must train my children, yes that is what I will do. I will speak kindly to them, and their mother too; abandon that pattern that was once my life. Though it may be hard, I will seek counsel from the Lord.
The cycle this time has two wheels as we play.
The parents teach by example not with dread
and the children, honor their parents and willingly be led.

Oh, What A Friend

During my life I'd had some friends, some were good to hang around, but some on my face put a frown. Oh, to have a friend like that, they would shoot the bullet and stab you in the back. One over a spat, would end your life. In the blink of an eye, they wouldn't care who for you, would cry.

No, they wouldn't think twice, and with your life, they would gladly pay the price.

But know this for sure, a choice is always made left or right, to go shoot hoops or start a fight.

We are in this life one to one, working together is a lot more fun.

If the answer is wrong, or we miss the hoop, we get a second try, no parent for their child would have to cry.

Kindness and laughter are the key to replacing the thoughts in our heads -the overpowering thoughts that we dread.

In this world of Covid vaccination, murmuring words and hidden faces, keep our backs against the wall.

Our actions are the key to helping a friend, like you and me no matter the color we may be.

A Healthy Fear

A person that does not obey God
is missing out on greatness.
We must learn, we must grow.
In order to climb to the top,
We must fall on our knees, it is in
the Lord that strength is gained.
Fearing the Lord is a blessing to the ears,
not all ways dreading what He will do.
He's not waiting to harm -His arms
are stretched out wide waiting to be our guide.
So, like a cheetah protects her cubs, and
the little ones watch but are not alarmed.

Likewise, The Almighty God, keeps those that are His safe from harm. He is a Lion, and we are His pride. His pride are those that trust in Him as their guide. He is not a terror, to His pride; but a loving Savior that protects and guides. And by this we learn to embrace "A healthy fear."

Family Day

This is the day families come together.

It doesn't matter about the weather.

Snow, rain, or high gale, this family's love somehow prevails.

We sing, talk, and act out scenes,

and some recite rhymes on what this day means.

After all the acting and playtime is done, we group together and have dinner as one.

And once we separate and head our separate ways; we laugh as we give God the praise, for another well-planned day with the family.
No need to be in despair, if my earthly family isn't there.
God's family is everywhere.
Every time the church meets the family of God takes a seat.
No matter, 3 feet or 6 feet apart, yes Covid has taken its toll, but we are all the family of God, the very young and the old.

Teachable

Small, cute, and cuddly.
Easily molded and shaped.
But if left to this world, cute and cuddly becomes
oversized, unattractive, and hard.
But with care love and guidance,
rough become smooth, kind
words spoken
heal broken spirits,
gentle touches calm a weary heart.
Teaching and healing become everyone's part.

FAITH

Faith is the substance of things hoped for and the evidence of things not seen.
Hebrew 11:1
You have faith, my friend, let me show
you know how this is so, every time the winter comes, you believe that it will snow.
Snow is the action fulfilling your belief.
You have faith that the sun will heat in the warm months like June and springtime will bring scented blooms.
Our Lord has put us here so we can enjoy this earth, while putting His Son first.
So, let's practice our faith, it is here in Jesus'
name. Because it is for us to this earth he came.

Parting The Mind

Part the mind with the foolish,
and birds of prey will feast.
Words spoken will change,
your words will never look the same.
Part the mind with the wise
and your soul will be at rest, and
your words will give strength to all
those that hear
like marrow to bones.

SIMPLICITY

Oh, haughty and pharisaic like man,
God will confound
you with simplicity.
So instead, of bragging and standing
tall just because you can, do this instead-
bend down grab a towel
and lend a helping hand.

SPIRITUAL, NOT PHYSICAL

A foolish man and a wise man conversed.
The topic—how will you serve Him now? (Come along and learn of the master).
We have destroyed your churches and all knowledge
of your God.
We have burned your books and your bibles.
We have beaten everyone that calleth on your God.
Now who will you turn to and where will you go?
Ha-ha, how will you know his will?
The reply—
"Oh, vain and perverse man, child of the devil,
yes, you have destroyed our buildings, but
not our churches.
We that belong to Christ are the Church.
Yes, you have burned our books.
But hear this, wicked one,
I can learn of God's gentleness when I see
a delicate butterfly, as it flutters through the sky.

I can see his strength as I observe the mighty Oak tree,
her borders are wide, and her roots are deep into the earth.
I can hear his songs of love, when I listen to birds' love calls.
I can see and be humbled by his might—as Redwoods bow down to the Lord at the blow of his nostril. You did mention that you have burned the bibles; ha-ha,
His word I have hid in my inward parts that I may not sin against him.
I know His word and it is pure, holy and true.
You see, I am prepared because our war is spiritual, not physical.

God's Natural Flow

When it rains, God's love is shown.
He rids the desert of its harsh dry sand for a season.
His love is truly the reason.
Night into day, day into night, and out of the dust springs beautiful flowers,
grass grows and water-filled the once dusty ground.
Animals race to the water hole, and live.
They drank water with their family, where water was not.
Each animal drinks, they know their spot.
Enemies raced to the very same hole.
They know life is in that watery ground,
and if only for a moment, their passions are contained-
contained for a minute but not forevermore.
Watch GOD's creation when the rain starts to beat
against the earth.
If you are in despair, focus on God's love.
His love is in the natural things that are around.
On your face, you'll find a smile overtaking your frown.
Listen, even the animals experience the joy of birth and the despair of
watching family become earth.
Despair will come, and despair will go
but focus on the Lord and watch his "Natural Flow."

Have A Heart

Oh, how weak, how great is my despair; my mind is so heavy.
It's like an unliftable stone, and I'm a weary traveler.
Who can lift this stone from my heart? I have lost the seed of man.
Man's seed has torn from my womb and fled into the sea,
with it went my heart. So, if you have a heart, please give it to me so my pain
would cease.
In my Lord's Day, I would have rented my garment and covered in sackcloth
and ashes from this broken heart
and all the world would know my pain.
And would stand in the town square asking- Have you a heart?

Section II

PERSONAL WORDS OF GRATITUDE

FROM THE HEART WITH YOU IN MIND

(FAMILY AND FRIENDS)

To Lizzie M. Wynn

I've finally realized that the only card that can set forth my feelings for you is the one that I write myself.
First thing, I love you mom, and appreciate all you have done for me.
Dot Wynn, I've searched high and
low to come up with one word to describe you, according to me,
that word is "sustain."
Mom, you are a sustainer.
You supplied me with necessities and nourishment when I was an infant.
You provided for me when I was a young child.
You supported me from below and kept me from falling when I was an adolescent.
You supported my broken spirit with resolution.
You encouraged me when I was a young man.
You bear up under the daily pressures of motherhood
with love and understanding.
Now that I am a man,
I realize that it is hard to raise a family.
But with you and daddy as my example, you both helped me through.

MOTHER

In you the Lord has chosen to place the river of life.

Many have poured out from that river, and I am thankful that I am one of them. You rose above your motherly duties and have cared for and cradled many; and from their infancy, you have taken them in with few complaints, but with an abundance of compassion and love.

Mama because of you, I've learned to love the unlovable and to accept the unacceptable.

This day and always, I'll give honor to you because to you honor is due.

To My Grandmother and Friend

It's not difficult to see how important a parent-child
relationship is.
I'm experiencing unconditional love for the child the Lord has given me.
Often, I glance out of my window and sigh. I don't know if you realize the
love that I have for you.
You've preserved my room for me for many years.
It is still a private place where I can recline and collect my thoughts at the
close of each day.
And when I need something as
Insignificant as tweezers,
I know just where to look.
On those countless occasions we leave our child in your care, there was never
a need to worry or despair.
In him, you are building character and strong values he'll need in this life
and to succeed.

COMING TOGETHER

How long has it been? Three, four, five years ago?
All I know is that I've missed you, my loyal and loving friend.
White has overpowered my dark locks, but that is just a testament to the years I've seen.
And the smile in my heart is a testament to the joy those years brought.
How pleasing it is to have a friend like you in my life.
We have shared ups and downs and life's many uncertain times.
Coming together with you brought renewed meaning to my life.
We used to greet the sun and welcome the moon.
Yes, do you remember we used to talk from morning till noon?
Five years seems like a lifetime, but to experience this feeling after five years would be grand but if nine years are granted to me than nine years I will wait. I will wait for my dear friend, praying that I will see you again.

Daddy

It is the Lord that gives strength to your bones and prudence to your life. It is through his strength, that you have raised a family that is proud to call you Daddy.

Cherish the love

I overheard a conversation at the supermarket while shopping with David, my husband.
The conversation was between three women, and it went like this:
Hi Sue, hello Mary, how are you doing? I'm fine, they shared words, words, and friendly smiles; even a bit of laughter.
Mary introduced her husband to Sue and the tone changed.
Sue's expression and composure changed.
Sue said, John died.
My heart rushed, and I moved over to my husband.
I thought hmm, what would I do if he were to die first?
My eyes lifted and for a moment. I connected with the pain Sue harbored in her heart.
Sue continued, yes, he died three months ago, and I miss him so very much.
Mary was speechless, giving her grieving friend a moment to speak.
We left that area, but those words never left my heart. I remember the conversation well.
Cherish the love that we have today because today is all we have.

Precious Moments

Precious are the moments of childhood
this is understood.
Suddenly you had three trusting
children to raise alone.
Love was your motivation,
noble was your actions.
You placed us in a secure and loving home?
When I travel through
the closet of my memories.
I thank the Lord for your undying love
and determined mind.
And through it all, you have
proven to be a wonderful father and
a devoted friend.

The Taste Of Home

I tasted a cookie today, and it took me to the time that I skinned my knee, and your special touch helped lessen the pain.
I tasted a cookie today, and it reminded me of the peaceful hours of naptime. It resonates in my mind, it's just a memory.
I tasted a cookie today, and it reminded me of all the sweet aromas and delectable tastes of home.
Thank you for the memories
And for being the parent that you are.

I love you mom

Wonders of Life

The awesome beauty of
Monarch butterflies
come together far above the trees, as
the gentle breeze blows.
An expectant mother takes
care of her baby while the
baby is still in her womb.
A father bonding with his son.

No Matter What

Struggles in life.
What your friends are struggling with may not bring you down; you might even consider their actions foolish and trivial; you might not want them around.
But as sure as the stars are affixed between the heavens and the earth, you too- my friend, will encounter
your own struggles,
and worries seemingly without end.
Please take courage and don't despair.
Keep God's name forever in the frontal lobe of your mind and meditate on his divine word.
Give thanks always, no matter what
and he will direct your paths.
And when the walls of life rise on both sides,
search your heart and the divine Holy Spirit will guide you, with the word.
Follow–like a ravenous rabbit following a bunch of carrots out of a maze. He protects the unaware ill prepared rabbit from the pack of crouched wolves.
You will make it, just follow the guide.

Dearest Mother

Mother, you are special, and your love is real.
You selected a delicate flower from an abundant field.
Love was your motivation.
A young child, such as I was-
did not understand that love
takes the form of a firm hand.
Now that I am no longer home
your guidance rings crystal clear.
Now your words are as precious as stones,
and I often yearn to be back at home.
Yes mama, you are dear to me
and may the Lord's grace guide
your way, till the close of your day.

TWINS

Born on the same day just moments apart. I don't quite comprehend how we have the same thoughts, though we are miles apart.
I feel your joy, and when you are blue,
I just got to believe that you feel mine too. I felt the skip in your heart, when I mentioned dad. You know he visited,
me from his near-by pad.
Twins yes, though this is true,
we are as different as each day is new.
The country is where you chose to stay.
Mating calls of crickets are at the close of your day.
My home is in the city, and I'm having a blast.
But I have learned that traveling to work is quite a task.

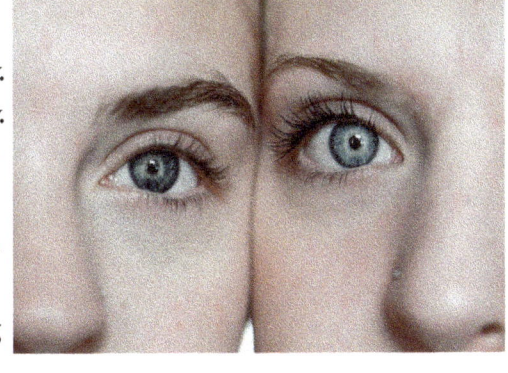

But despite our differences this is true, there's no one I'd rather call sister but you.

WE ARE ONE

You are flesh of my flesh and bone of my bone
Genesis 2:23
My heart and eyes are forever fixed on the Father because he answers all prayers, and it's in him and through him that our love will grow. Please remember even when times are hard, and laughter is rear-
You are flesh of my flesh and bone of my bones.
Flesh does not separate at a break or tear; it is cleaned, and balm is applied, and the healing begins.
And you are flesh of my flesh and bone of my bone; we are one. The trials and tears are from the hurt and pain that break and tear at the bond we share.
The balm is the Father's love that heals and calms, by His Holy name. I invite all to take this God into your home and welcome his grace. And young men everywhere can say to their wives, you are bone of my bone and flesh of my flesh.
We are one.

A Father's Day Wish For My Brother

We are woven from the fibers of our mother's womb,
 my brother and me.
We are strength for our sons and confidence for our daughters,
 my brother and me.
We are the source of life in our homes, respect is given- respect is received,
 my brother and me.
I thank the Lord for you
 on this Father's Day.
You are a loving father and a wonderful man,
 and you should know that you bring comfort to your home.
My brother.

Raging Storms

The raging storms life presents today
Raging storms have come our way.
The storms that have trampled our parents in the past have raised their heads in our lifetime.
Hmm, and we are perplexed, and we wonder will they last?
No one can answer that yea or nay,
but the word of the Lord will keep us through our days or until we fade away.
If this storm is passed to our children and they will get to ask us, why is this happening to me anyway? Then we can remember that we asked the same questions with curious looks, and worried eyes.
It offers us the time to reflect and say hmm, the storm won't last this too, will pass.

Cry If You Must

As you drown in pain so deep
it's no wonder you can't sleep.
Rest your head on God's pillow of clouds.
On his clouds you can whisper, scream, and cry out loud.
Yes, cry out loud. There is one that knows your pain, he suffered more and even the same.
Peter denied him in a crowd. He even cursed and screamed out loud. Judas sold him for thirty pieces of silver,
this caused Judas' heart to quiver; thus, Judas' life was lost, and our Savior died on the cross.
When he arose, he was seen by many. Thomas was not at the resurrection, but the Lord's mercy is true.
He suffered an unbelieving Thomas to thrust his hand in his side; and to fill the nail prints in his hand. The Lord's mercy made Thomas a believing young man.
So, fear not, but cry if you must.
But give praise and honor to him.
He erases all doubt and replace victory where there is defeat and fears.
Yes, he wipes away all tears.

Teens of the '90s

Being a teen in the '90s, some will have you believe that this is impossible to achieve.
Cheer up, though it might be hard, keep your eyes on the Lord.
Beware of those that put things in their nose and skin,
and say this is the only way to be in with the crowd.
Allow me to enlighten your mind, to fight for what is right,
this is a worthy fight.
Not the fight with fist or hands. This fight is about values, intellect, and skills.
You are training to know when to act, talk, be quiet and be still.
At times you will go against what you know is right. But keep pushing and know–time gives way to experience,
and experience develops skills, skills give way to knowledge and knowledge gives purpose and purpose produces strength.
And when others see how strong you have come, rejoice!
Know your spiritual life has just begun.
Look around there may be a teen with their head hanging down.
What will you do to erase their frown?

Drop A Tear/and Rise With Praise

Drop a tear for our youth today.
Their plight in life is a long and artificial way.
Is this the plight of the youth alone?
No, most of society sings the same song.
A small case of pills is blamed when young girls fall to the motherly way, they say that darn pill let me down, or there's just not enough drug stores in this part of town.

Weapons are used to solve problems or to settle a dispute. A party is held because the job was done, that is artificial fun.
So, drop a tear for the youth today and let us always and forever to the Lord pray.
But life does not stop with some choices, challenges are certain we know that is true.
Stress can drape our minds, but we need not fear.
A single grain of sand causes great irritation in a shell but with love and care, it holds in its grip a beautiful and costly pearl.
So, tears may fall and that's okay,
Struggles amidst of love will save the day, as we kneel on our knees and pray.

Section III
IT'S ALL ABOUT LOVE

Riley My Love

Faith happened when I stopped thinking. I thought life was empty, and though I searched for answers, none came through.
So, I fell on my Knees and sought The Lord in prayer. I felt for an answer, but my ears were dull, and I could not hear, and my eyes were weary, and I could not see. I was in total despair, but just when I stopped hoping, caring or dreaming.
A ray of hope caught my eye... It was you my darling, it was you.
I knew that when our eyes met, I knew that I wanted you in my life. And now, wow look at what the Lord has done. I am not just Anastasia your friend, but now I am Anastasia Ramsey your wife.

Frank

I am yours.
Frank, you know my dear, hmm ... you are the love of my life.
Only if you knew just how much I've prayed to be your wife.
Ravenous and uncultured desire is what lives in my soul.
Your unselfish acts and caring ways attract Victoria and that creates stories to behold. Olivia sparkled and gleamed at your sight.
Unfailing love is what awaits us.
My African Prince Frank.
From Princess Stephanie
Your wife.

My Love

I think about the sunshine that fills the room
when you are present, then I think of you.
I think about the beautiful family that the
Lord has given us, then I think of you.
Know this my darling, you are loved,
and I'm thinking of you.
The Lord is good, and I thank Him for you.

When I Say, "I Love You"

I love you more and more each day, even when friction comes to our home to play.
There are countless reasons why my affection rests with you and rises when you rise.
When I say, "I love you,"
It is because of those almond-colored eyes; they beckon me in a crowded room.
It is because of your strength, which swallows me whole when we embrace.
It is because of your ebony skin, which enhances all of you that is tangible.
It is because you let me keep my feline when you felt my pain. It is because you love the Lord, and you allow his word to guide your path.
It is because you are teaching our offspring how to give their first fruit to the Lord before giving to themselves.
Yes, for all these reasons and more, from the highest mountain, my love cries out.
I say to you:
Honey, I am proud to be your wife.

GREAT FATHER AND HUSBAND

My love for you grows deeper and deeper still, every day.
The Lord that sent you my way will be my Lord forever.
To say that you are special is not enough,
essential to my life is what you are.
Our Father, who is in Heaven, knew what I needed.
Your tenderness and patience cushion me when I fall,
and when I succeed your love and favor encourages me to reach the next level.
You are the love of my life and a power that drives me to succeed. You are
the absorbent fabric that wipes my tears when I cry, and you are the cushion
that catches me when I fall.
Growing with you is a journey that I would do again and again.
You are the love of my life, my husband and friend.

Being Married Is An Oxymoron

Marriage at its finest it will take you in flight, a whisper in the ear: I have finally got it right!
Marriage will cause disappointment, in direct opposition to delight, burned toast, worked late, oh yeah, we are married, that's just great!
You will laugh with happiness and frown, tears streaming to the ground. Sometimes you won't no one around!
Marriage at a glance, will take your breath away, holding one another you will thank the Lord for the day.
The oh-so fine and handsome groom that took the time to ask for your hand. The beautiful bride, her fitted gown, and the most fragrant bouquet in all the land.
Marriage tells you to leave, to stay, you are in my way! It screams; it is quiet hush! I have nothing to say. It makes your heart race, palms sweat, red in the face. Look at how beautiful you look, your mind pace. Marriage makes you want to be immersed into Christ,
His Word is filled with truths that keep a marriage alive, and
still, you seek counsel from family and friends. You pray that this joy will never end. Marriage makes you bite your lip not once but twice.
Marriage says, why did I take your advice?
Just because you are sleek, curvy, built, or round, I can't be controlled. I won't be bound.
Marriage exposes love for what it is.
I am not tangible; I am more than what you feel.
Those gorgeous, deep brown eyes, curvy hips, and subtle smiles.

Marriage is captivating like a bird's feather falling from on high. As we walk through this hilly valley or watery ground, we can thank the Lord for the blessing we have found. This is my story, it's true.
What does your marriage mean to you?

A Thought On This Mother's Day

Mothers are the ones that wipe away tears, stay up at night, and calm your fears.
Mothers read the books and drive the vans, made popsicles from broccoli and beets, and said to their children—
here's a tasty treat.
And when you are feeling lonely and full of despair but your face mask a look of grace, and you say that you are fine,
mothers stop and bow to say a prayer,
with the assurance that God's grace, love, and mercies are everywhere.

Trusting in The Lord

Let's see, trusting in the Lord, well for a Godly mother, that's what I do.
As I gaze into the written word and repeat to my children what I have seen, experienced, heard, and read from your divine word.
I lift my head with both joy and a sigh, to the Lord of peace, love, and grace. A great calm overwhelmed my mind because I know that through my work as a mother, he has always been my guide.
I love the Lord and the blessings that he laid in my arms. And though one has departed from this life, he will never depart from my thoughts or my heart.
I will carry on as a mother of two oh Lord, what else am I to do?
For I carry on, only in You.

My Prayer

When I kneel to pray night after night, I petitioned the Lord
I want to be a wife.
I could have asked the Lord for a man that is handsome, kind, and bright.
I could have said, Lord let him be a devoted family man, one that would work for his family and with us he would make plans.
But instead, night after night and day after day I asked the Lord to send a God-fearing man my way.
Though the Lord on high grants no wishes, his promises are true.
He says, seek matters of heaven and things that are true, and many blessings will come to you.
This my dear husband this is true, everything that I have asked is found in you.

Let Them Wonder

Let them wonder and gaze at the morning, eve and night sky,
as you cook by the moonlight before they close their eyes.

But as your child starts to move around and wonder, leaping, sliding, and digging as they explore, or sing morning till noon- just think of this as their job. As they practice and get better and better.

As they kick balls and toss balls through the hoops or practice music lessons on the piano or a flute; let them hear you say, job well done, even when they have just begun.
Oh, I see that you are sad- let them hear these words from mom and dad.
And let them head out and explore some more. Mom and dad, with you by their side, encouraging and motivating them gleaming with delight. They will want to try again and again. This is their homework, and you are their fun.
Their growth and development have begun.
What else is childhood for?

Section IV
From My Children
David Wynn II

THE GREAT CALM

Jesus was teaching but he became tired.
He told his disciples about his desire.
Across the lake, they went to rest their heads.
Jesus asleep, disciples awoke.
Massive storm erected.
In horror, the disciples awoke the Lord.
Disciples plead to the Lord to help.
The Lord got up and made the storm obey and calmed the wind.
And asked, "Where is your faith?"
The fearful disciples said,
"What manner of man is this?
For he commanded even the winds and water,
and they obey him."
Oh, to be like the wind and the waves.

From the Pen of Sheila Wynn
Fluttering Thoughts

Honestly, these things just come in and out of
my head whenever they please. I get ideas out of nowhere and
for some odd reason, they seem to go away when they are wanted most.
Ask me why I did this or come up with a plan to do the most innovative
thing, I would say I don't know.
They say to take a minute and think
I try,
And try,
And try,
I still will not have a clue.
At that point, I will get frustrated with myself.
Trying to figure out why or how I did something.
The thought just comes and goes.

Poem by Rachel Wynn
Love Grows Like A Garden

My mom is the best mom,
Bet yours isn't as spectacular.
Even though she is as loud as a tom-tom.
She always makes me laugh with her peculiar ways.
She's a poet, a comedian, a therapist, a star,
A teacher, a nurse, even when you fall and get a scar.
She always wants for us better than she had,
Though it doesn't always seem that way.
Living in this world and seeing all the bad,
now she teaches us and guides us how
to live each day.
My mother is a proverb 31 kind -of lady.
She speaks wisdom, cares for her
house, and protects all her babies.
I love her sooo much and I hope that she knows,
Just like her lovely garden, my love will always grow.

Dearest mom
10 things I want you to know
by: Nicole Wynn

1. I get much of my creativity from you
2. I love you
3. I am thankful for your knowledge and encouragement.
4. I love you
5. I'm thankful that you taught me how to treat others and my siblings.
6. I love you.
7. For the record, you've got the greenest thumb in the whole house.
8. I love you.
9. You mean so much to me.
10. 10.And I love you, enjoy your day.

From Sabrena
A word of Appreciation

I know that I appreciate all the time
spent with you.
All the time spent helping me
to improve.
Mom, I may not show it but,
I need to hear your loud call down
the hall and warm reminders of
my chores.
Happy am I that you trained me on
how to work with the babies,
I will recall those skills someday.
I love and appreciate you,
mom, in every way.

FROM CHELSEA
YOU BRING PASSION INTO ALL
THAT YOU DO

You are incredible, whether it be
learning scriptures, poetry, child
development, or being a mom. You
bring passion.
Do you sleep?
I feel your love all the time.
You've shown me how much you care
And I am forever thankful, and I
love, love, love you.
Mom

Section V
It is The LORD

The Footprints of Jesus

The footprints of Jesus are visible,
not invisible as man supposed.
Not hard to see,
made by God
fearing parents like you and me.
As we follow God's instructions
and follow his plan
We tread the road for our children
as God commands.
In Proverbs 22:6
We are to- train up our children
in the way
they should go, (thus said
The Lord),
When they are old,
they will not depart from it.
So, we kindle the fire as we
teach because.
Proverb 127:3,4
Children are indeed an inheritance
from the Lord.
And the fruit of the womb
is the reward.
Like arrows in the hands of
a warrior,
so are children born in
one's youth.
What an amazing responsibility
we have, as parents.
We kindle the fire between
God and man.
There's power in being a parent
and a righteous command given to
Sons and daughters of man
that is a wonderful course
charted by God,
and given to man, as he has trusted
us to carry out His plan.

The Wind's Door

I have seen the doors the wind goes through–all the rooms are side by side.
I've seen the doors that the wind goes through- the mountains peek and the valleys are deep, and the desert sand keeps them parched and dry.
Fresh white, black and brown sand smears and spread wherever it will.
But when the Lord whispers, be still, go to your room, each grain obeys on the mountain top they lay. Some meet with the heat as they obey and take their seat. They rest high above the ground not making a sound.
I saw the place where the wind rests, bringing frost on the mountain top and chill to its peeks.
I have seen the place where the wind rest and it's breathtaking at best.

THE CLOUDS DO CRY

Clouds bumping and sliding no wonder they cry, bumping as they fill and prepare to weep.
The immature one's rush to mom and dad, but hold on before you know it, they will be grown as the wind push and say, time to grow as they bump and fill with rain, saying not a word but they cry just the same. Just a puff a minute ago, yet another part of the natural flow. This amazing sight is not from man, it's truly part of The LORD's plan.

Sprinkles of Salt

Salt sprinkles-
As we moved swiftly through the air sprinkles of salt were everywhere. Pecks were high clear enough to view from the sky. Trails traveled to no end then as the mountains peck, the ground give way to canyons so deep.
I wonder what they would say, if they could speak?
Would they talk about the parched feeling, as they lay open in the earth unprotected from the sun? Would it rant and rave about the precarious winds that picks up its children and tosses them around to neighboring parts reconstructing the land? No, the wind lifts and lands at God's command.
Oh, sons and daughters deep in the land. Will you rejoice as puffs of clouds swell overhead turning darker and darker as it swells and expand? Does it breathe with excitement anticipating being filled and nourished? The great cavity breathes in with excitement and out with somber, and says, I am a part of God's holy and divine plan.
I have been sprinkled at His command.

THE FLAT LAND SPEAKS

Flat land says, what about me? I am steadier and sound. The All mighty allow His children to build on me. But I can be shaken, yes, I can. When the sun rises high up in the sky, my cracks can be wide and deep. And when I sneeze or take a deep breath and crumble and bake in the heat. There is a thing called a quack, it opens me up wide and turns structures aside- causing land dwellers to run and hide. Land dwellers says it's due to the folk in the land. But the land tremble at God's command.

The End

I want to thank all my readers for taking the journey through the collection of visual and poetic art,

in my book, "Inspirational Winds."

CONTRIBUTORS:

Sabrena Wynn -Graphic art
Sheila Wynn- Art placement
Chelsea Wynn- Poem
Sabrena Wynn-Poem
Nicole Wynn-Poem
Rachel Wynn-Poem
David Wynn II-Poem
Sheila Wynn Poem

My Husband David
Love and encouragement

www.ingramcontent.com/pod-product-compliance
Lightning Source LLC
LaVergne TN
LVHW061625070526
838199LV00070B/6586